spicy
pad
c   g

William W. Wongso and Hayatinufus A.L. Tobing

A delightful selection of the most popular Indonesian dishes—including the all-time favorite Beef Rendang, Spicy Grilled Chicken and Beef Satays—perfect for entertaining the fiery hot Padang-style.

PERIPLUS

Asam gelugor are dried slices of garcinia fruit that impart a sour flavor to dishes. *Asam gelugor* should be soaked in water to soften and rinsed before added either whole or sliced to other ingredients. If not available, replace with tamarind juice.

Banana leaf (*daun pisang*) is indispensable as a food wrapper, used to wrap food for steaming or grilling. The moisture within the banana leaf makes a difference to the texture and flavor of the food. Fresh banana leaf should be softened for easy folding before wrapping food in it, either by soaking it in hot water for 5 to 10 minutes or briefly heating it over low flame. If not available, replace with aluminium foil.

Candlenuts (*kemiri*), also known by its Malay name *buah keras*, are waxy, round cream-coloured nuts from the fruit of the candlenut tree. They are usually ground and added to sauces and spice paste for texture and flavor. Candlenuts should only be eaten after proper preparation. One method is to dry-roast the nuts over medium heat until they can be cracked open, then stir-fry the crushed kernels with other ingredients such as garlic, shallots and shrimp paste. Such a mixture is often used as a flavoring ingredient in Indonesia and most of Southeast Asia. Store in the refrigerator as candlenuts turn rancid quickly. Raw macadamia nuts can be used as substitutes.

Cardamom (*kepulaga*) is a pungent spice commonly used to perfume rice dishes, curries, cakes and desserts. Pale green, straw colored or black, the cardamom pods enclose about 15 to 20 intensely fragrant brown or black cardamom seeds. Available as powder, seeds or whole pods, the best flavor is achieved by using the seeds removed from the pod directly. Ready-ground cardamom is not recommended as it loses its fragrance very quickly. Cardamom pods should be stored in a tightly-sealed jar to preserve their aroma.

Chilies (*cabai*) are indispensable in Padang cooking and many different varieties are used. The large moderately hot, finger-length green, red or yellow chilies are the most commonly used. **Green chilies** are the unripe fruits and have a flavor different from ripe red chilies. **Dried chilies** of this variety are also used in some dishes. They should be soaked in warm water to soften before grinding or blending. Hottest of all chilies are the tiny bird's-eye chilies. As with all chilies, wash your hands thoroughly after handling and discard seeds for reduced heat.

Cloves (*cengkeh*) are

small, brown, nail-shaped spice usually added whole to curries for flavor and aroma. Buy cloves whole or ground. For best flavor, grind your own using the "buds" only.

Coconut cream and **coconut milk** (*santan*) are used in many Asian desserts and curries. To obtain fresh coconut cream (which is normally used for desserts), grate the flesh of 1 coconut into a bowl (about 4 cups of grated coconut flesh), add $1/2$ cup water and knead thoroughly a few times, then strain with a muslin cloth or cheese cloth. **Thick coconut milk** is obtained by the same method but by adding double the water to the grated flesh (about 1 cup instead of $1/2$ cup). **Thin coconut milk** (which is used for curries rather than desserts) is obtained by pressing the coconut a second time, adding 1 cup of water to the same grated coconut flesh and squeezing it again. Although freshly pressed milk has more flavor,

coconut cream and milk are now widely sold canned or in packets that are quick and convenient.

Coriander (*ketumbar*) is one of the most commonly used spices in Southeast Asia. The whole plant is used—the root, stem and leaves. The seeds are roasted and then ground in a spice mill and often used together with white pepper and cumin in curry pastes. **Coriander leaves**, also known as cilantro or Chinese parsley, have a distinctive smell and attractive appearance and are used for their fresh flavor, and as a garnish. Coriander root is a popular Thai seasoning. For storage, wash and dry the fresh leaves before placing them in a plastic bag in the refrigerator—they will keep for 5 to 6 days.

Cumin are similar in appearance to caraway seeds. Dark brown and ridged on the outside, the seeds are often roasted and ground before using. The earthy aroma is distinct. Its flavor is often likened to liquorice.

Dried shrimp paste (*trassi*) or belacan in Malay, is a dense mixture of fermented group shrimp. It is sold in dried blocks and ranges in color from pink to blackish-brown. Shrimp paste should be slightly roasted to enhance its flavor before adding to other ingredients. Traditionally, it is wrapped in banana leaves and roasted over embers for a few minutes. Now it is commonly roasted directly over low flame using tongs for 30 seconds or heated in a skillet, wrapped in aluminium foil, for 1 to 2 minutes. Alternatively it can also be microwaved very quickly in a bowl covered with plastic for 30 seconds or so. Do not overcook the shrimp paste or it will scorch, become bitter and hollow.

Galangal (*laos*) is a rhizome similar to ginger in appearance and a member of the same family. Known as *kha* in Thailand and *lengkuas* in Singapore and Malaysia, this aromatic root is used to flavor curries in much of Southeast Asia. Dried galangal lacks the fragrance of fresh galangal, and most food stores now sell it fresh. It can be sliced and kept sealed in the freezer for several months.

Kaffir lime is a small lime that has a very

knobby and intensely fragrant skin, but virtually no juice. The skin or rind is often grated and added to dishes as a seasoning. The fragrant **kaffir lime leaves** (*daun jeruk perut*) are used whole or finely shredded in some Padang dishes, giving a wonderfully tangy taste to these dishes. Fresh leaves are available in most grocery stores and wet markets. Store fresh leaves in the freezer.

Lemongrass (*serai*), also known as citronella, is a lemon-scented stem which grows in clumps and is an important spice in flavoring curries and sauces. Each plant resembles a miniature leek. Use only the thicker bottom one third of the lemongrass stem. Remove and discard the dry outer leaves and use only the tender inner part of the plant. Lemongrass is available fresh, frozen or

dried; fresh lemongrass is preferable because of its stronger smell and flavor.

Palm sugar is made from the distilled juice of various palm fruits (especially the coconut and arenga palms). Palm sugar varies in color from gold to dark brown. It has a rich flavor similar to dark brown sugar, molasses or maple syrup, which make good substitutes.

Pandanus leaves, also known as pandan leaves or screwpine leaves, are long thin leaves used to impart a delicate fragrance and sweet, grassy flavor into rice, cakes and desserts. They are also used as wrappers for seasoned morsels, cakes and desserts. Though they can be deep-frozen, always look for fresh leaves at the supermarkets. A few drops of bottled pandan or vanilla essence is a good substitute.

Petai beans (*buah petai*), also known as parkia beans or stinkbeans, are strong-smelling green beans sold either in the pod (about ten beans to a pod) or ready shelled and usually split in half lengthwise. Believed to be good for the kidneys and liver, *petai* beans may be eaten raw or cooked.

Potato patties for use in Beef Noodle Soup and Potato Patties (*Soto Daging*) on page 24: mash 350 g (12 oz) boiled potatoes; add 1 tablespoon deep-fried shallots and $1/_2$ teaspoon salt, shape into 8 small patties, dip in beaten egg and pan-fry in oil until golden brown.

Salam leaf (*daun salam*)

is a large, dark green leaf that is added to curries. Rarely encountered outside Indonesia, it has no direct substitute and may be omitted if not available.

Sour carambola fruits (*belimbing wuluh*) are small pale green acidic fruits grow in clusters on the carambola tree. A relative of the sweeter starfruit, sour carambola fruits are used whole or sliced to give a sour tang to some soups, fish dishes and sambals. Sour grapefruit or tamarind juice can be used as a substitute.

Tamarind (*asam Jawa*) is a sour fruit that comes in a hard pod shell. Commonly available in the form of pulp, it can

be bought fresh or dried. Tamarind juice is one of the major souring agents in most Southeast Asia cooking. To make tamarind juice, mix 1 tablespoon dried tamarind pulp with 2 tablespoons warm water to soften, then mash well and strain to remove any seeds and fibers (see *asam gelugor*).

Turmeric (*kunyit*) is a member of the ginger family. This rhizome has a very rich yellow interior (which can stain clothing and plastic utensils) and an emphatic flavor. When fresh it resembles ginger but it is usually sold in yellow powder form. When fresh tumeric is not available, substitute $1/_2$ teaspoon turmeric powder for 2 cm ($1/_2$ in) fresh turmeric. Fresh turmeric leaves are also used in Padang cooking as a herb.

Spicy Potato Crisps (Keripik Kentang Balado)

Oil for deep-frying
1 kg (2 lbs) potatoes,
  thinly sliced
1 sprig celery, leaves only,
  sliced, to serve

Spice Paste
5 to 6 red chilies, sliced
5 shallots
2 tablespoons oil
1 teaspoon sugar
5 tablespoons freshly
  squeezed lime juice
1 teaspoon salt

1 Heat the oil in a wok over medium heat until hot. Deep-fry the potato slices until crispy and golden brown, 2 to 3 minutes. Remove and drain on paper towels. Set aside.

2 To make the Spice Paste, grind the chilies and shallots to a smooth paste in a mortar or blender. Heat the oil in a wok over medium low heat, stir-fry the paste until fragrant, about 3 to 5 minutes. Add the sugar and lime juice, and stir-fry for another 1 to 2 minutes, then add the salt and mix well.

3 Reduce heat to low, add the potato crisps and mix thoroughly until well coated, about 5 minutes. Remove from heat and sprinkle with celery leaves before serving.

Serves 4
Preparation time: **20 mins**
Cooking time: **20 mins**

Sambal Eggplant (Taruang Balado)

3 tablespoons oil
750 g (1 1/2 lbs) Asian
  eggplants, halved
  lengthwise

Sambal Paste
5 red chilies, sliced
5 shallots
2 tablespoons oil
1 large or 2 small toma-
  toes, deseeded, flesh
  coarsely chopped
1 tablespoon freshly
  squeezed lemon or
  lime juice
1 teaspoon salt

Serves 4
Preparation time: **15 mins**
Cooking time: **15 mins**

1 Make the Sambal Paste first by grinding the chilies and shallots to a smooth paste in a mortar or blender. Heat the oil in a wok or skillet over medium low heat, add the paste and stir-fry for 3 to 5 minutes until fragrant. Add the tomatoes and stir-fry until soft, then season with the lemon or lime juice and salt. If the paste is too thick, dilute with 2 to 3 tablespoons of water. Remove and set aside.

2 Heat the oil in a wok or skillet and fry the eggplants over medium heat until tender, 2 to 3 minutes each, turning to brown both sides. Remove and drain the excess oil.

3 Transfer the eggplants to a serving dish. Spread the Sambal Paste on top and serve hot with steamed rice.

Mixed Vegetables in Spicy Coconut Milk
(Gulai Sayur Campur)

250 g (9 oz) lean topside beef
1 liter (4 cups) water
$1/_2$ teaspoon salt
250 g (9 oz) young jackfruit, flesh cut into bite-sized pieces
150 g (5 oz) long beans, cut into lengths to yield 2 cups
5 large cabbage leaves, coarsely chopped to yield 2 cups
500 ml (2 cups) thick coconut milk
1 turmeric leaf
3 kaffir lime leaves
1 stalk lemongrass, thick bottom part only, tough outer layers discarded, inner part bruised

Spice Paste
2 candlenuts, crushed and dry-roasted
2 red chilies, sliced
5 to 6 shallots
2 to 3 cloves garlic
$2^1/_2$ cm (1 in) turmeric, peeled and sliced
$2^1/_2$ cm (1 in) galangal root, peeled and sliced
$2^1/_2$ cm (1 in) ginger, peeled and sliced
1 teaspoon salt

When cutting the jackfruit, leave the immature seeds intact; use an oiled knife to prevent any sticky sap from clinging to the blade.

Serves 4 to 6
Preparation time: **30 mins**
Cooking time: **2 hours**

1 Bring the beef, water and salt to a boil over high heat in a saucepan. Reduce heat to low, cover and simmer 1 to $1^1/_2$ hours until the beef is tender. Remove and set aside to cool, then slice the beef into small pieces.

2 To make the Spice Paste, grind all the ingredients to a smooth paste in a mortar or blender, adding some beef stock to keep the paste turning if necessary. Transfer to a bowl and set aside.

3 Return the beef to the beef stock and add the jackfruit pieces. Add some water if the beef stock is insufficient to just cover the beef and jackfruit. Bring the mixture to a boil over high heat, then reduce heat to medium, cover and simmer for about 15 minutes, until the jackfruit is tender and cooked. Add the Spice Paste and all the other ingredients, mix well and bring to a boil. Reduce heat to low and simmer uncovered for 10 to 15 minutes until the vegetables are cooked. Remove from heat, discard the turmeric leaf and lemongrass, and serve immediately.

Green Chili Sambal (Sambal Lado Mudo)

Oil for deep-frying
25 g (1 cup) dried *ikan bilis* or *ikan teri (*whitebait)*, heads discarded, soaked in warm water to soften and drained
5 shallots, sliced
10 green chilies, coarsely chopped
1 medium green tomato, deseeded, flesh diced
2 kaffir lime leaves, sliced
1 to 2 teaspoons sugar
1 teaspoon salt
3 tablespoons water
2 tablespoons freshly squeezed lime juice

1 Heat the oil in a wok until hot. Deep-fry the *ikan bilis* over medium heat until golden brown and crispy, 2 to 3 minutes. Remove and drain on paper towels. Set aside.

2 In a wok or skillet, heat 2 tablespoons of the oil over medium heat. Add the shallots and stir-fry until fragrant and translucent, about 1 minute. Add the chilies, tomato, lime leaves, sugar and salt, and stir-fry for 3 to 5 minutes. Add the water and simmer for about 3 minutes, then stir in the lime juice and remove from heat.

3 Transfer to a serving dish and spread the deep-fried *ikan bilis* on top. Serve immediately.

Serves 2
Preparation time: **15 mins**
Cooking time: **15 mins**

Cabbage in Coconut Milk (Gulai Manis)

500 ml (2 cups) thick coconut milk
5 to 6 shallots, thinly sliced
2 red chilies, thinly sliced
2 *salam* leaves (page 5)
5 cm (2 in) galangal root, peeled and sliced
1 teaspoon salt
500 g (1 lb) Chinese cabbage, coarsely sliced
3 eggs

Serves 4 to 6
Preparation time: **15 mins**
Cooking time: **20 mins**

1 Bring the coconut milk, shallots, chilies, *salam* leaves, galangal and salt to a boil over medium heat in a large saucepan, then simmer uncovered, stirring constantly, for about 5 minutes.

2 Stir in the Chinese cabbage and mix well. Simmer uncovered for about 10 minutes, until the cabbage is tender. Finally add the eggs, one at a time, waiting for each to set before adding the next egg. Mix well, remove from heat and serve immediately.

Cassava Leaves in Spicy Coconut Milk

500 ml (2 cups) beef stock or 1 beef stock cube in 500 ml (2 cups) hot water
100 g (3 oz) rump or topside steak, very thinly sliced
1 turmeric leaf
2 kaffir lime leaves
1 stalk lemongrass, thick bottom part only, tough outer layers discarded, inner part bruised
1 slice *asam gelugor* (dried garcinia fruit), soaked in warm water to soften
200 g (4 cups) young cassava leaves or 500 g (6 cups) spinach leaves
375 ml (1$^1/_2$ cups) thick coconut milk
40 g ($^1/_2$ cup) fresh *ikan bilis* (whitebait), rinsed and drained (optional)

Spice Paste
3 to 4 red chilies, sliced
4 shallots
3 cloves garlic
1$^1/_2$ cm ($^1/_2$ in) galangal root, peeled and sliced
1$^1/_2$ cm ($^1/_2$ in) ginger, peeled and sliced
1$^1/_2$ cm ($^1/_2$ in) turmeric, peeled and sliced
$^1/_2$ teaspoon salt

1 To make the Spice Paste, grind all the ingredients to a smooth paste in a mortar or blender, adding a little beef stock to keep the paste turning if necessary. Set aside.
2 Heat the beef stock in a wok or large saucepan over high heat. Add the beef, turmeric leaf, lime leaves, lemongrass and *asam* slices, stir in the Spice Paste and bring to a boil. Add the cassava leaves or spinach and mix well. Reduce heat to medium, cover and simmer for 25 to 30 minutes. Finally stir in the thick coconut milk and *ikan bilis* (if using) and simmer until the sauce is thickened and the *ikan bilis* are cooked, about 10 minutes. Remove from heat and serve immediately.

Serves 4 to 6
Preparation time: **20 mins**
Cooking time: **40 mins**

Chicken Curry (Kalio Ayam)

4 tablespoons tamarind juice (page 5)
1 fresh chicken (about 1$^1/_2$ kg/3 lbs), cut into 12 pieces
1 stalk lemongrass, thick bottom part only, outer layers discarded, inner part bruised
2 kaffir lime leaves
1 turmeric leaf (optional)
1 liter (4 cups) thick coconut milk
1 teaspoon salt

Spice Paste
2 teaspoons coriander seeds, lightly roasted
6 to 8 red chilies, sliced
8 shallots
4 cm (1$^1/_2$ in) galangal root, peeled and sliced
4 cm (1$^1/_2$ in) ginger, peeled and sliced
2$^1/_2$ cm (1 in) turmeric, peeled and sliced

1 To make the Spice Paste, grind all the ingredients to a smooth paste in a mortar or blender, adding some coconut milk to keep the paste turning if necessary. Transfer to a bowl and set aside.
2 Pour the tamarind juice over the chicken pieces, mix well and marinate for at least 30 minutes.
3 Heat the Spice Paste in a wok over medium heat for 3 to 5 minutes until fragrant. Add the lemongrass, lime leaves, turmeric leaf (if using), coconut milk and salt, mix well and bring slowly to a boil. Reduce heat to low and simmer uncovered for about 10 minutes, stirring constantly. Finally add the chicken and simmer for another 30 to 35 minutes, stirring constantly, until the chicken is tender. Remove from heat and serve immediately with steamed rice.

You may use 750 g (1$^1/_2$ lbs) beef liver instead of chicken. Blanch the liver for 5 minutes, then drain and dice. Cook in the spicy coconut milk until tender .

Serves 4 to 6
Preparation time: **20 mins + 30 mins to marinate**
Cooking time: **45 mins**

Deep-fried Chicken (Ayam Goreng)

250 ml (1 cup) water
1 fresh spring chicken (about 1 kg/2 lbs), quartered, or 4 chicken thighs with drumsticks attached
2 slices *asam gelugor* (dried garcinia fruit), soaked in warm water to soften
Oil for deep–frying

Spice Paste
1 teaspoon black peppercorns
2 shallots
2 cloves garlic
$2^1/_2$ cm (1 in) ginger, peeled and sliced
1 teaspoon salt

Ikan Bilis Sambal
10 dried red chilies, soaked in warm water to soften, stems discarded, deseeded
1 small tomato, sliced
1 shallot
1 teaspoon dried shrimp paste, roasted (page 3)
$^1/_2$ teaspoon salt
2 tablespoons freshly squeezed lime juice
2 teaspoons oil
2 tablespoons Ikan Bilis Powder (see note)

1 To make the Spice Paste, grind all the ingredients to a smooth paste in a mortar or blender, adding some water to keep the paste turning if necessary. Transfer to a bowl and set aside.

2 To make the Ikan Bilis Sambal, combine the chilies, tomato and shallot in a heatproof dish and steam in a steamer until soft, about 10 minutes. Grind the steamed ingredients, dried shrimp paste and salt to a smooth paste in a mortar or blender. Transfer to a serving bowl, stir in the lime juice and oil, add the Ikan Bilis Powder and mix well. Set aside.

3 Bring the Spice Paste and water to a boil in a wok or large saucepan over high heat, stirring constantly. Add the chicken and *asam* slices, and mix well. Reduce heat to medium, cover the wok and simmer, turning the chicken several times, until the sauce has dried up and the chicken is cooked, about 30 minutes. Remove from heat, discard the *asam* slices and pat dry the spiced chicken with paper towels.

4 Heat the oil in a wok over medium heat until very hot. Deep-fry the spiced chicken until golden brown on both sides, about 5 minutes. Remove and drain on paper towels. Serve with the bowl of Ikan Bilis Sambal on the side.

To make the Ikan Bilis Powder, use 3 tablespoons of dried ikan bilis. Discard the heads and soak the ikan bilis in warm water until soft, then drain. Dry-fry the ikan bilis in a wok or skillet over low heat until crispy, 5 to 10 minutes, then grind to a powder in a mortar or grinder.

Serves 4
Preparation time: **30 mins**
Cooking time: **45 mins**

Green Duck Curry
(Gulai Hijau Itik)

2 tablespoons freshly squeezed lime juice
1 fresh duck (about 2 kg/4^1/$_2$ lbs), cut into
   12 to 14 pieces
2 tablespoons oil
1 liter (4 cups) water
5 kaffir lime leaves
1 or 2 turmeric leaves
2 stalks lemongrass, thick bottom part only, tough
   outer layers discarded, inner part bruised

Spice Paste
2 teaspoons black peppercorns
8 candlenuts, crushed and dry-roasted
10 to 15 green chilies, sliced
4 shallots
5 cm (2 in) galangal root, peeled and sliced
2^1/$_2$ cm (1 in) ginger, peeled and sliced
2^1/$_2$ cm (1 in) turmeric, peeled and sliced
1 teaspoon salt

1 To make the Spice Paste, grind all the ingredients to
a smooth paste in a mortar or blender, adding some
water to keep the paste turning if necessary. Transfer
to a bowl and set aside.
2 Rub the lime juice onto the duck pieces. Set aside
for 15 minutes.
3 Heat the oil in a wok over medium heat and stir-fry
the Spice Paste until fragrant, 3 to 5 minutes, then add
the water and bring to a boil, stirring constantly. Add
the duck, lime leaves, turmeric leaves and lemongrass,
and mix well. Simmer uncovered, turning the duck
pieces frequently, until the duck is tender and the
curry thickens. This should take about 1 hour.
Remove from heat and serve with steamed rice.

Serves 6 to 8
Preparation time: **30 mins**
Cooking time: **1 hour 15 mins**

Spicy Grilled Chicken
(Singgang Ayam)

375 ml (1 1/2 cups) thick coconut milk
1 fresh spring chicken (about 1 kg/2 lbs), split along
  the breast, opened and flattened
1 turmeric leaf
5 kaffir lime leaves
2 stalks lemongrass, thick bottom part only, tough
  outer layers discarded, inner part bruised

Spice Paste
1 tablespoon black peppercorns
3 to 4 shallots
2 cloves garlic
2 1/2 cm (1 in) galangal root, peeled and sliced
2 1/2 cm (1 in) turmeric, peeled and sliced
1 cm (1/2 in) ginger, peeled and sliced
1 to 2 teaspoons sugar (optional)
1 teaspoon salt

1 To make the Spice Paste, grind all the ingredients to
a smooth paste in a mortar or blender, adding some
coconut milk to keep the paste turning if necessary.
Transfer to a bowl and set aside.
2 Heat the Spice Paste in a wok over medium heat and
gradually stir in the coconut milk. Bring the mixture
slowly to a boil and simmer for 3 to 4 minutes, stirring constantly. Add the chicken, turmeric leaf, lime
leaves and lemongrass, and mix well. Cover the wok
and simmer for about 30 minutes, turning the chicken
frequently, until the chicken is tender. Remove from
heat.
3 Grill the spiced chicken on a charcoal or pan grill
over medium heat until golden brown on both sides,
basting with the leftover sauce. This should take about
5 minutes. Cut the grilled chicken into serving pieces
and serve hot.

Serves 4
Preparation time: **20 mins**
Cooking time: **45 mins**

Ayam Pop with Red Sambal

1 fresh chicken (about 1 $^1/_2$ kg/3 lbs), skin removed
   and discarded, cut into 4 pieces
5 tablespoons oil, for frying
Shrimp crackers (*krupuk*), to serve

Red Sambal
5 red chilies, sliced
5 to 6 shallots
2 tablespoons oil
5 kaffir lime leaves
1 medium tomato, cut into wedges
1 teaspoon salt
1 tablespoon freshly squeezed lemon or lime juice

Sauce
2 $^1/_2$ cm (1 in) ginger, peeled and sliced
2 cloves garlic, minced
$^1/_2$ teaspoon white peppercorns
1 teaspoon salt
250 ml (1 cup) water

1 To make the Red Sambal, grind the chilies and shallots to a smooth paste in a mortar or blender. Heat
the oil in a wok or skillet over medium heat, stir-fry
the paste and lime leaves until fragrant, 3 to 5 minutes.
Add the tomato and stir-fry for 2 to 3 more minutes.
If the mixture gets too dry, dilute it with some water.
Season with the salt and lemon or lime juice and remove
from heat. Transfer to a serving bowl and set aside.
2 Bring the Sauce ingredients to a boil over high heat in
a wok or large saucepan and continue to boil for 5 minutes. Reduce heat to medium, add the chicken, cover
and simmer for 20 to 30 minutes. Remove and pat dry
the chicken pieces with paper towels.
3 Heat the oil in a wok or skillet and fry the chicken
pieces for 2 to 3 minutes on each side, until light
brown. Remove and drain on paper towels. Serve hot
with shrimp crackers and Red Sambal.

Serves 4
Preparation time: **20 mins**
Cooking time: **45 mins**

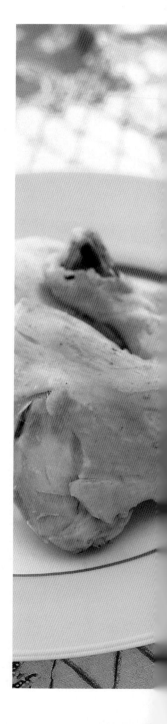

Beef Noodle Soup with Potato Patties
(Soto Daging)

500 g (1 lb) lean topside beef
2 tablespoons oil, for frying
250 g (9 oz) dried glass noodles, soaked in warm water to soften
2 to 3 hard-boiled eggs, quartered lengthwise
2 spring onions, sliced
2 tablespoons Crispy Fried Shallots (see note)

Marinade
1 teaspoon salt
2 stalks lemongrass, thick bottom part only, tough outer layers discarded, coarsely chopped
5 kaffir lime leaves, chopped
4 cm (1$^1/_2$ in) galangal root, bruised
2$^1/_2$ cm (1 in) ginger, bruised
1 cinnamon stick (8 cm/ 3 in)

Sambal
10 red chilies, sliced
$^1/_4$ teaspoon salt

Soup
1 teaspoon black peppercorns
3 shallots
2 to 3 cloves garlic
2 tablespoons oil
2$^1/_2$ liters (10 cups) beef or chicken stock

Accompaniments
1 lime, quartered
8 small potato patties (page 5)
Deep-fried sago wafers (optional)

1 Combine all the ingredients for Marinade in a large bowl and mix well. Place the beef in the Marinade and marinate for at least 4 hours or overnight if possible.
2 To make the Sambal, grind the chilies and salt to a smooth paste in a mortar or blender. Transfer to a small serving bowl and set aside.
3 To make the Soup, grind the peppercorns, shallots and garlic to a smooth paste in a mortar or blender, adding a little beef or chicken stock to keep the paste turning if necessary. Heat the oil in a stockpot over medium heat and gently stir-fry the paste until fragrant, 3 to 5 minutes. Add the beef or chicken stock, increase heat to high and bring to a boil. Remove and set aside.
4 Pat dry the marinated beef with paper towels. Heat the oil in a wok or skillet over medium heat until hot, fry the beef until cooked, turning to brown both sides, 5 to 10 minutes. Remove and drain the excess oil. When cool, thinly slice the beef.
5 To serve, briefly blanch the glass noodles and transfer to a serving bowl. Add the Soup, top with fried beef slices and eggs, sprinkle with spring onions and Crispy Fried Shallots. Serve hot with Sambal and Accompaniments.

To make the Crispy Fried Shallots, thinly slice several shallots as desired and stir-fry in a few tablespoons of hot oil over low heat for 1 to 2 minutes, stirring constantly, until golden brown and crispy. Remove with a slotted spoon and drain on paper towels.

Serves 4 to 6
Preparation time: **30 mins + 4 hours marination**
Cooking time: **25 mins**

Lamb Curry (Gulai Cincang)

3 tablespoons oil
5 to 6 shallots, thinly
   sliced
1 cinnamon stick (8
   cm/3 in)
250 g (9 oz) lamb ribs,
   cut into lengths
750 g (1 1/2 lbs) boneless
   lamb, cut into pieces
1 teaspoon salt
2 slices *asam gelugor*
   (dried garcinia fruit),
   soaked in warm water
   to soften
1 liter (4 cups) thin
   coconut milk
250 ml (1 cup) thick
   coconut milk

Spice Paste
1 tablespoon coriander
   seeds
1 teaspoon black
   peppercorns
1/2 teaspoon cumin
1/4 teaspoon nutmeg
   powder
3 cloves
2 cardamom pods, split
   open to obtain seeds
4 candlenuts, crushed
8 to 10 red chilies, sliced
4 to 5 cloves garlic
2 1/2 cm (1 in) ginger,
   peeled and sliced
2 1/2 cm (1 in) turmeric,
   peeled and sliced
2 1/2 cm (1 in) galangal
   root, peeled and sliced

1 To make the Spice Paste, dry-fry the coriander seeds, peppercorns, cumin, nutmeg, cloves, cardamom seeds and candlenuts in a wok or skillet over low heat until fragrant, 5 to 10 minutes. Remove and grind to a powder in a mortar or spice grinder. Transfer to a bowl and set aside. Grind all the other ingredients to a smooth paste in a mortar or blender, adding some coconut milk to keep the paste turning if necessary. Remove and combine with the ground spice in the bowl, and mix until well blended. Set aside.

2 Heat the oil in a wok over medium heat and stir-fry the shallots and cinnamon until golden brown, 1 to 2 minutes. Add the Spice Paste and stir-fry until fragrant, 3 to 5 minutes. Add the lamb, salt, *asam* slices and thin coconut milk, mix well and bring to a boil. Reduce heat to low and simmer uncovered for 10 to 15 minutes, stirring constantly, until the lamb is tender and the curry is thickened. Add the thick coconut milk and stir well. Increase heat to medium and bring the curry to a boil, then simmer for 2 more minutes before removing from heat.

3 Serve immediately with steamed rice.

Serves 4 to 6
Preparation time: **30 mins**
Cooking time: **30 mins**

Spicy Beef Stew
(Pengek Daging)

750 g (1 1/2 lbs) lean topside beef, cut into bite-sized chunks
1 or 2 turmeric leaves
5 kaffir lime leaves
3 slices *asam gelugor* (dried garcinia fruit), soaked in warm water to soften
1 teaspoon salt
3/4 to 1 liter (3 to 4 cups) water
20 basil leaves

Spice Paste
3 candlenuts, crushed and dry-roasted
8 to 10 red chilies, sliced
3 to 4 shallots
4 cloves garlic
1 1/2 cm (1/2 in) ginger, peeled and sliced
1 1/2 cm (1/2 in) galangal root, peeled and sliced
1 1/2 cm (1/2 in) turmeric, peeled and sliced

1 To make the Spice Paste, grind all the ingredients to a smooth paste in a mortar or blender, adding some water to keep the paste turning if necessary. Transfer to a bowl and set aside.
2 Place the Spice Paste, beef chunks, turmeric leaves, lime leaves, *asam* slices and salt in a saucepan, and add enough water to just cover the beef. Mix well and bring to a boil over high heat. Reduce heat to low, cover the saucepan and simmer until the sauce is thick and the beef is very tender, 30 minutes to 1 hour. Remove from heat and stir in the basil leaves just before serving.

Serves 4
Preparation time: **20 mins**
Cooking time: **1 hour**

Beef Rendang (Rendang Daging)

1½ liters (6 cups) thick coconut milk
1 turmeric leaf
5 kaffir lime leaves
2 stalks lemongrass, thick bottom part only, outer layers discarded, minced
2 slices *asam gelugor* (dried garcinia fruit), soaked in warm water to soften
1 kg (2 lbs) lean topside beef, cut into bite-sized chunks

Spice Paste
10 to 15 red chilies, sliced
5 to 6 shallots
4 cloves garlic
2½ cm (1 in) galangal root, peeled and sliced
1½ cm (½ in) ginger, peeled and sliced
1½ cm (½ in) turmeric, peeled and sliced
1 teaspoon salt

1 Make the Spice Paste first by grinding all the ingredients to a smooth paste in a mortar or blender, adding some coconut milk to keep the paste turning if necessary. Transfer to a bowl and set aside.

2 Heat the Spice Paste in a wok over medium heat for 3 to 5 minutes until fragrant, then gradually stir in the coconut milk. Add the turmeric leaf, lime leaves, lemongrass and *asam* slices, mix well and bring to a boil. Reduce heat to low, simmer uncovered for 2 minutes, stirring constantly to prevent curdling.

3 Add the beef chunks and continue to simmer uncovered until the beef is tender, and the sauce has almost dried up. This should take 1 to 1½ hours. Add some water if the sauce has dried up before the beef is cooked. Finally reduce heat to very low and stir-fry the beef chunks until they brown in the oil from the coconut milk, taking care not to scorch the beef. Remove from heat, discard the *assam* slices, turmeric and lime leaves if desired, and serve hot with steamed rice or coconut rice.

If preferred, you may use dried red chilies instead of fresh red chilies. Discard the stems of the dried red chilies, deseed and soak in warm water to soften before using.

Serves 4 to 6
Preparation time: **20 mins**
Cooking time: **1 hours 45 mins**

Beef Satays (Satai Daging)

1 kg (2 lbs) beef loin or rump, diced
3 tablespoons oil
1 to 1 1/4 liters (4 to 5 cups) water
20 to 25 bamboo skewers (see note)
3 tablespoons rice flour
1 tablespoon sago or tapioca flour
1 tablespoon oil, for grilling
Crispy Fried Shallots (page 24), to garnish

Marinade
1 turmeric leaf
4 kaffir lime leaves
1 stalk lemongrass, thick bottom part only, tough outer layers discarded, inner part bruised
2 slices *asam gelugor* (dried garcinia fruit), soaked in warm water to soften
2 teaspoons salt

Spice Paste
1 tablespoon coriander seeds
1/2 teaspoon cumin
1 teaspoon freshly ground black pepper
8 red chilies, sliced
3 to 4 shallots
2 to 3 cloves garlic
2 1/2 cm (1 in) galangal root, peeled and sliced
2 1/2 cm (1 in) turmeric, peeled and sliced
2 1/2 cm (1 in) ginger, peeled and sliced

1 Combine all the ingredients for Marinade in a large bowl. Place the beef cubes in the Marinade, mix well and marinate for at least 4 hours or overnight if possible.

2 To make the Spice Paste, dry-fry the coriander seeds and cumin in a wok or skillet over low heat until fragrant, 5 to 10 minutes. Combine with all the other ingredients and grind to a smooth paste in a mortar or blender, adding some water to keep the paste turning if necessary.

3 Heat the oil in a wok over medium heat and stir-fry the Spice Paste until fragrant, 3 to 5 minutes. Add the marinated beef cubes and 750 ml (3 cups) of the water and bring to a boil, then cover and simmer until the beef is tender, about 1 hour. Remove the beef from the beef stock and thread 3 to 4 cubes onto each bamboo skewer. Thread all the beef cubes in this manner.

4 To make the dipping sauce, strain the beef stock to remove the lemongrass, *asam* slices, turmeric and kaffir lime leaves. If there is insufficient stock, add about 250 ml (1 cup) of the water. Combine the rice flour, sago or tapioca flour and 4 tablespoons of the water in a saucepan, mix well and stir in the beef stock, then bring slowly to a boil over medium heat, stirring constantly. Reduce heat to low and simmer uncovered for 10 to 20 minutes, stirring continuously, until the sauce is thickened. Transfer to a serving bowl and set aside.

5 Brush the satays with a little oil and grill, a few at a time, on a charcoal or pan grill over medium heat for about 3 minutes on each side, until cooked. Arrange on a serving dish and sprinkle with Crispy Fried Shallots. Serve hot with the dipping sauce.

The bamboo skewers should be soaked in water for at least 1 hour before using to keep them from burning. In Sumatra, this dish is usually prepared with 750 g (1 1/2 lbs) mixed offal such as tripe, intestines and heart, and 250 g (1/2 lb) brisket beef.

Makes 20 to 25 sticks
Preparation: **30 mins + 4 hours to marinate**
Cooking time: **2 hours**

Spicy Simmered Beef
(Gulai Gadang)

$^3/_4$ to 1 kg (1$^1/_2$ to 2 lbs) lean topside beef, in one piece
2 stalks lemongrass, thick bottom part only, tough outer
   layers discarded, inner part bruised
3 kaffir lime leaves
2 turmeric leaves
3 slices *asam gelugor (*dried garcinia fruit), soaked in
   warm water to soften
$^3/_4$ to 1 liter (3 to 4 cups) water

Marinade
6 candlenuts, crushed and dry-roasted
8 to 12 red chilies, sliced
3 shallots
1 to 2 cloves garlic
2$^1/_2$ cm (1 in) ginger, peeled and sliced
2$^1/_2$ cm (1 in) turmeric, peeled and sliced
1 to 2 teaspoons salt

1 Make the Marinade first by grinding all the ingredients to a smooth paste in a mortar or blender, adding some water to make the paste turning if necessary. Transfer to a large bowl, add the beef, mix until well coated and marinate for 30 minutes to 1 hour.
2 Place the marinated beef, lemongrass, lime and turmeric leaves and *asam* slices in a saucepan just large enough to hold the mixture, and add enough water to cover. Bring the mixture to a boil over high heat, then reduce heat to medium, cover and simmer for about 1 hour, stirring constantly, until the beef is very tender and the sauce is thick. Remove from heat and discard the lemongrass, lime and turmeric leaves, and *assam* slices.
3 Slice the beef just before serving.

If asam gelugor is not available, *replace with 4 table-spoons of tamarind juice (see page 2 and 5).*

Serves 4 to 6
Preparation time: **15 mins + 30 min marination**
Cooking time: **1 hour**

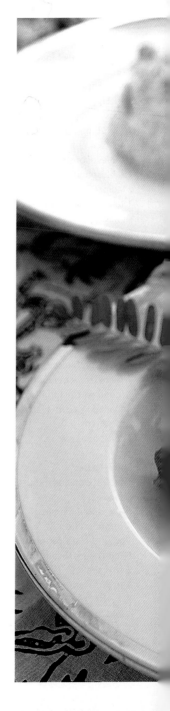

Dried Beef with Chili Dressing (Dendeng Balado)

2 tablespoons freshly squeezed lime juice
1 teaspoon salt
750 g (1$^1/_2$ lbs) lean topside beef, thinly sliced
  along the grain
Oil for deep-frying

Chili Dressing
2 to 3 tablespoons oil
4 shallots, sliced
8 to 10 red chilies, coarsely chopped
7 kaffir lime leaves
$^1/_2$ teaspoon salt
3 to 4 tablespoons freshly squeezed lime juice

1 Rub the lime juice and salt into both sides of the beef slices and dry in the sun, turning several times, until completely dried on both sides. Alternatively, dry the beef in an oven over very low heat for 3 to 4 hours.
2 To make the Chili Dressing, heat the oil in a wok or skillet over medium heat. Stir-fry the shallots until fragrant and translucent, 1 to 2 minutes. Add the chilies and lime leaves, and stir-fry for 2 to 3 minutes until the chilies are tender. Season with the salt and lime juice, and mix well. Transfer to a serving bowl and set aside.
3 Heat the oil in a wok over medium heat until very hot. Deep-fry the dried beef, a few at a time, until brown and very crispy, 3 to 5 minutes each. Remove and drain on paper towels.
4 Spread the Chili Dressing over the deep-fried beef slices if desired and serve with the bowl of Chili Dressing on the side.

Serves 4 to 6
Preparation time: **20 mins + drying**
Cooking time: **20 mins**

Beef Jerky (Dendeng Batokok)

1 kg (2 lbs) lean topside beef, in one piece
1 teaspoon tamarind pulp
3 kaffir lime leaves
1 teaspoon salt
500 to 750 ml (2 to 3 cups) water
4 tablespoons oil
1 to 2 medium green tomatoes, chopped, to garnish

Spice Paste
6 to 8 green chilies, sliced
2 unripe medium green tomatoes, deseeded
3 shallots
1 teaspoon salt
2 tablespoons freshly squeezed lime juice

1 To make the Spice Paste, pulse the chilies, tomatoes and shallots several times to chop finely in a mortar or blender. Transfer to a large bowl, add the salt and lime juice, mix well and set aside.

2 Place the beef, tamarind pulp, lime leaves and salt in a saucepan. Add enough water to just cover the beef and bring to a boil over high heat. Reduce heat to medium, cover and simmer for 1 to $1^1/_2$ hours, stirring occasionally, until the beef is tender. Remove and set aside to cool.

3 Slice the beef along the grain into thin slices. Pound each slice with a mallet or the back of a cleaver to tenderise, then place it on a plate and sprinkle a little oil over both sides. Grill the beef slices on a charcoal or pan gril over medium heat for 3 to 5 minutes on each side, until cooked.

4 Add the grilled beef to the bowl of Spice Paste and gently toss to mix well. Transfer to a serving dish and garnish with chopped green tomatoes.

Serves 4 to 6
Preparation time: **20 mins**
Cooking time: **2 hours**

Beef and Liver Stew
(Gulai Kancah)

500 g (1 lb) brisket beef, cut into bite-sized chunks
2 slices *asam gelugor (*dried garcinia fruit), soaked in
  warm water to soften
2 stalks lemongrass, thick bottom part only, tough
  outer layers discarded, inner part bruised
3 kaffir lime leaves
1 turmeric leaf
750 ml (3 cups) water
300 g (10 oz) beef liver, cut into bite-sized chunks

Spice Paste
1 teaspoon black peppercons
12 to 15 dried red chilies, soaked in warm water to
  soften, stems discarded, deseeded
5 to 6 shallots
3 cloves garlic
$2^1/_2$ cm (1 in) galangal root, peeled and sliced
$2^1/_2$ cm (1 in) ginger, peeled and sliced
$2^1/_2$ cm (1 in) turmeric, peeled and sliced
1 teaspoon salt

1 To make the Spice Paste, grind all the ingredients to
a smooth paste in a mortar or blender, adding some
water to keep the paste turning if necessary.
2 Place the Spice Paste, beef, *asam* slices, lemongrass,
lime and turmeric leaves in a saucepan. Add enough
water to cover the beef and bring to a boil over high
heat. Reduce heat to medium, cover and simmer for
about 30 minutes, stirring occasionally. Add the beef
liver and continue to simmer for another 30 minutes
until the beef and liver are tender, adding some water
if the sauce dries up before the beef is cooked.
Remove from heat, discard the *assam* slices and
lemongrass, and serve the stew with steamed rice.

Serves 4 to 6
Preparation time: **25 mins**
Cooking time: **1 hour**

Fish Curry (Gulai Ikan)

2 tablespoons freshly squeezed lime or lemon juice
1 teaspoon salt
750 g (1 $^1/_2$ lbs) fish fillets or cutlets
1 liter (4 cups) thick coconut milk
1 turmeric leaf
3 kaffir lime leaves
1 stalk lemongrass, thick bottom part only, tough outer
  layers discarded, inner part bruised
2 slices *asam gelugor* (dried garcinia fruit), soaked in
  warm water to soften
12 lemon basil leaves

Spice Paste
6 to 8 dried red chilies, soaked in warm water to
  soften, stems discarded, deseeded
3 to 4 shallots
2 cloves garlic
2 $^1/_2$ cm (1 in) galangal root, peeled and sliced
2 $^1/_2$ cm (1 in) ginger, peeled and sliced
2 $^1/_2$ cm (1 in) turmeric, peeled and sliced

1 Make the Spice Paste first by grinding all the ingredients to a smooth paste in a mortar or blender, adding some coconut milk to keep the paste turning if necessary. Transfer to a bowl and set aside.
2 Rub the lime or lemon juice and salt onto both sides of the fish fillets. Set aside for about 15 minutes, then rinse and drain.
3 Heat the Spice Paste in a wok or large skillet over medium heat. Stir in the coconut milk and add the turmeric leaf, lime leaves, lemongrass and *asam* slices. Bring the mixture slowly to a boil, then simmer uncovered for 3 minutes, stirring constantly. Add the fish and continue to simmer until the fish is cooked, 6 to 10 minutes depending on the thickness of the fish fillets. Remove from heat and stir in the basil leaves before serving.

Serves 4
Preparation time: **20 mins**
Cooking time: **20 mins**

Ikan Bilis with Petai Beans (Goreng Badar Petai)

Oil for deep-frying
250 g (9 oz) dried *ikan
bilis* or *ikan teri (*whitebait*)*, heads discarded,
soaked in warm water
to soften and drained
20 *petai* beans, halved
lengthwise
1 tablespoon freshly
squeezed lime juice
1 to 2 teaspoons sugar

Spice Paste
8 to 10 dried red chilies,
soaked in warm water to
soften, stems discarded,
deseeded
3 to 4 shallots
$^{1}/_{2}$ teaspoon salt

1 To make the Spice Paste, grind all the ingredients to a smooth paste in a mortar or blender. Transfer to a bowl and set aside.
2 Heat the oil in a wok over medium heat until hot. Deep-fry the *ikan bilis* until golden brown and crispy, 2 to 3 minutes. Remove and drain on paper towels. Set aside.
3 Heat 2 tablespoons of the oil in a wok or skillet over medium heat. Stir-fry the Spice Paste and *petai* beans until fragrant and cooked, 4 to 5 minutes. Add the deep-fried *ikan bilis*, season with the lime juice and sugar, and mix well. Remove from heat and serve as an accompaniment.

Serves 4 to 6
Preparation time: **15 mins**
Cooking time: **15 mins**

Spicy King Prawns (Udang Balado)

2 tablespoons freshly
  squeezed lime juice
1 teaspoon salt
750 g (1 1/2 lbs) fresh
  large prawns, peeled
  with tails intact and
  deveined
Oil for deep-frying
20 *petai* beans, halved
  lengthwise

Seasoning
10 red chilies, sliced
5 shallots
1 medium tomato,
  deseeded
1 to 2 teaspoons sugar
  (optional)
1 teaspoon salt

1 To make the Seasoning, pulse all the ingredients in a mortar or blender several times to chop finely, but do not turn into a paste. Transfer to a bowl and set aside.
2 Rub the lime juice and salt onto the prawns. Set aside for 15 minutes, then drain the prawns and pat dry with paper towels.
3 Heat the oil in a wok over high heat until very hot. Deep-fry the prawns, a handful at a time, until just cooked, about 1 minute each. Remove and drain on paper towels.
4 Heat 3 tablespoons of the oil in a wok or skillet over medium heat. Stir-fry the *petai* beans with the Seasoning until fragrant and cooked, 4 to 5 minutes. Add the deep-fried prawns and mix until well blended, taking care not to overcook the prawns. Remove and serve immediately.

Serves 4
Preparation time: **15 mins**
Cooking time: **15 mins**

Squid Curry (Kalio Cumi-cumi)

750 g (1 1/2 lbs) fresh squids (6 to 7 medium squids)
750 ml (3 cups) thick coconut milk
3 slices *asam gelugor* (dried garcinia fruit), soaked in warm water to soften
3 kaffir lime leaves
1 stalk lemongrass, thick bottom part only, outer layers discarded, inner part bruised
1/2 teaspoon salt
Sprigs of lemon basil leaves, to serve

Spice Paste
10 red chilies, sliced
5 to 6 shallots
4 cloves garlic
2 1/2 cm (1 in) galangal root, peeled and sliced
2 1/2 cm (1 in) turmeric, peeled and sliced
2 1/2 cm (1 in) ginger, peeled and sliced
1 teaspoon salt

1 To make the Spice Paste, grind all the ingredients to a smooth paste in a mortar or blender, adding some coconut milk to keep the paste turning if necessary. Transfer to a bowl and set aside.

2 Rinse each squid thoroughly, detaching and discarding the head. Remove the cartilage in the center of the tentacles. Peel the reddish-brown skin from the body sac and scrape the inside of the body sac with the dull edge of a knife. Rinse well, slice the body sac into rings. Set aside.

3 Heat the Spice Paste in a wok or saucepan over medium heat and stir in the coconut milk. Add the *asam* slices, lime leaves, lemongrass and salt, mix well and bring to a boil. Simmer uncovered, stirring constantly, until the curry is thickened, about 8 minutes. Add the squids and simmer until just cooked, 2 to 3 minutes. Remove from heat, sprinkle with basil leaves and serve hot with steamed rice.

Serves 4 to 6
Preparation time: **20 mins**
Cooking time: **15 mins**

Detach the head of each squid and remove the long transparent quill from the body sac.

Squeeze to remove the cartilage in the center of the tentacles.

Fish and Cassava Leaves Steamed in Banana Leaf (Palai Bungkus Daun Ubi Kayu)

1 tablespoon freshly
squeezed lime juice
2 teaspoons salt
500 g (1 lb) boneless fish
fillets, cut into bite-
sized pieces
5 to 6 sour carambola
fruits, thinly sliced
250 ml (1 cup) thick
coconut milk
2 turmeric leaves, very
thinly sliced (optional)
150 g (3 cups) young
cassava leaves, blanched
until soft and drained,
divided into 4 portions
1 large banana leaf, softened (page 2) and cut
into four 20-cm (8-in)
squares, for wrapping
8 toothpicks

Spice Paste
10 red chilies, sliced
5 to 6 shallots
4 cloves garlic
2$^1/_2$ cm (1 in) turmeric,
peeled and sliced
1 teaspoon salt

1 To make the Spice Paste, grind all the ingredients to a smooth paste in a mortar or blender, adding some coconut milk to keep the paste turning if necessary. Transfer to a bowl and set aside.

2 Rub the lime juice and 1 teaspoon of the salt onto the fish fillets and set aside for 15 minutes, then rinse and drain.

3 Rub the remaining salt onto the carambola slices. Set aside for 5 minutes, then rinse and drain.

4 Combine the Spice Paste, seasoned fish fillets, salted carambola slices, coconut milk and turmeric leaves (if using) in a large bowl and mix until well blended.

5 Divide the fish mixture into 4 equal portions. Place each portion onto the center of a piece of banana leaf and top with 1 portion of the cassava leaves.

6 To wrap the filling with the banana leaf, fold the square piece of banana leaf in half to enclose the filling, then fold the corners inward at both ends and fold each end towards the center to form a package, fastening the folded ends with toothpicks. Repeat with the remaining ingredients to make 4 packages altogether.

7 Place the packages in a steamer and steam until cooked, about 15 minutes. Serve hot.

Serves 4
Preparation time: **30 mins**
Cooking time: **15 mins**

Place the fish mixture on a square piece of the banana leaf and top with the cassava leaves.

Fold the square piece of banana leaf in half to enclose the filling.

48

Fold the corners inward at both ends.

Fold each end towards the center and fasten with toothpicks.

Steamed Carp with Spices and Vegetables
(Pangek Ikan Mas)

150 ml (²/₃ cup) thick coconut milk

2 tablespoons tamarind juice (page 5)

1 teaspoon salt

1 fresh carp (about 1 kg/2 lbs), cleaned

4 large pieces banana leaf, for steaming

1 stalk lemongrass, thick bottom part only, tough outer layers disarded, sliced

4 kaffir lime leaves

1 turmeric leaf

5 to 6 sour carambola fruits, sliced lengthwise (optional)

10 lemon basil leaves

150 g (5 oz) long beans, cut into lengths to yield 2 cups

5 large cabbage leaves, coarsely chopped to yield 2 cups

Spice Paste

5 candlenuts, crushed and dry-roasted

10 red chilies, sliced

5 to 6 shallots

2¹/₂ cm (1 in) turmeric, peeled and sliced

2¹/₂ cm (1 in) galangal root, peeled and sliced

2¹/₂ cm (1 in) ginger, peeled and sliced

1 teaspoon salt

1 To make the Spice Paste, grind all the ingredients to a smooth paste in a mortar or blender, adding some coconut milk to keep the paste turning if necessary. Transfer to a bowl and stir in the coconut milk, mix well and set aside.

2 Rub the tamarind juice and salt into both sides of the fish. Set aside for 15 minutes, then rinse and drain.

3 Line a wok with 2 pieces of the banana leaf, top with the fish, lemongrass, lime leaves, turmeric leaf, carambola slices (if using), basil leaves, long beans and cabbage. Spread the spiced coconut milk over the fish and vegetables, then cover with the remaining pieces of the banana leaf. Cover the wok and steam until the fish is cooked, about 20 minutes. Serve immediately.

Serves 4
Preparation time: **30 mins**
Cooking time: **20 mins**

Transfer the Spice Paste to a bowl and gradually stir in the thick coconut milk.

Spread the spiced coconut milk over the fish and vegetables before covering with the banana leaf.

Spicy Fish Curry (Gulai Ikan Cabai Rawit)

2 tablespoons freshly
squeezed lime or lemon
juice
1 teaspoon salt
750 g (1 1/2 lbs) fresh fish,
cleaned
750 ml (3 cups) thick
coconut milk
2 slices *asam gelugor*
(dried garcinia fruit),
soaked in warm water
to soften

Spice Paste
3 to 4 shallots
2 1/2 cm (1 in) turmeric,
peeled and sliced
1 teaspoon salt
7 to 8 bird's-eye chilies

1 Make the Spice Paste by grinding the shallots, turmeric
and salt to a smooth paste in a mortar or blender,
adding some coconut milk to keep the paste turning if
necessary. Add the bird's-eye chilies and pulse several
times to chop finely. Transfer to a bowl and set aside.
2 Rub the lime or lemon juice and salt onto both sides
of the fish. Set aside for 15 minutes, then rinse and drain.
3 In a wok, bring the Spice Paste and coconut milk
slowly to a boil over medium heat, then simmer
uncovered for 3 minutes, stirring constantly. Add the
fish and *asam* slices, and continue to simmer uncovered
for 6 to 10 minutes until the fish is cooked and the
curry is thickened. Remove and serve immediately
with steamed rice.

Serves 4 to 6
Preparation time: 20 mins
Cooking time: **15 to 20 mins**

Spicy Grilled Fish (Ikan Panggang)

4 to 6 fresh small mackerel, cleaned

1 stalk lemongrass, thick bottom part only, tough outer layers discarded, inner part bruised

Marinade
8 to 10 red chilies, sliced
2 to 3 shallots
$1^1/_2$ cm ($^1/_2$ in) ginger, peeled and sliced
$1^1/_2$ cm ($^1/_2$ in) turmeric, peeled and sliced
1 teaspoon salt
1 to 2 limes, peeled, deseeded and flesh chopped
200 ml ($^3/_4$ cup) thick coconut milk

1 To make the Marinade, grind the chilies, shallots, ginger, turmeric, salt and limes to a smooth paste in a mortar or blender, adding some coconut milk to keep the paste turning if necessary. Transfer to a wide bowl, stir in the coconut milk and mix well. Set aside.

2 Make 2 diagonal slits on each side of the fish. Place the fish and lemongrass in the Marinade, mix well and marinate for at least 30 minutes, spreading the Marinade over the fish several times.

3 Grill the marinated fish on a charcoal or pan grill over medium heat for 3 to 5 minutes on each side, basting frequently with the Marinade, until golden brown and cooked. Serve hot with steamed rice.

Serves 4
Preparation time: 20 mins + 30 mins marination
Cooking time: 20 mins

Fish Grilled in Banana Leaf (Palai Ikan)

1 whole fresh mackerel
  (750 g/1 $^1/_2$ lbs), cleaned
1 tablespoon freshly
  squeezed lime juice
2 teaspoons salt
6 to 7 sour carambola
  fruits, sliced (see note)
125 ml ($^1/_2$ cup) coconut
  cream
1 turmeric leaf, sliced
1 "cup leaf" (*daun
  mangkok*), sliced
  (optional)
2 large pieces banana leaf,
  softened (page 2), for
  wrapping
4 to 6 toothpicks

Spice Paste
5 red chilies, sliced
3 bird's-eye chilies
5 to 6 shallots
2 cloves garlic
2$^1/_2$ cm (1 in) turmeric,
  peeled and sliced
$^1/_2$ teaspoon salt

Serves 4
Preparation time: **30 mins**
Cooking time: **30 mins**

1 To make the Spice Paste, grind all the ingredients to a smooth paste in a mortar or blender, adding some coconut cream to keep the paste turning if necessary. Transfer to a bowl and set aside.

2 Make 3 diagonal slits on each side of the fish. Rub the lime juice and 1 teaspoon of the salt onto both sides of the fish. Set aside for 15 minutes, then rinse and drain.

3 Rub the remaining salt onto the carambola slices and set aside for 5 minutes, then rinse and drain.

4 Combine the Spice Paste with the coconut cream, salted carambola slices, turmeric and "cup leaf" (if using) in a large bowl and mix well.

5 Place the fish on a piece of banana leaf. Spread the Spice Paste mixture over the fish, making sure that the fish is coated well. Fold the banana leaf to wrap the fish securely, forming a package, then wrap the package with another layer of banana leaf, fastening with toothpicks if necessary.

6 Grill the fish on a charcoal or pan grill over medium heat for about 15 minutes on each side until cooked. Serve hot.

Trevally could be used instead of mackerel. To check if the fish is cooked, pierce with a knife; the flesh should be white right to the bone. If sour carambola fruits are not available, replace with the tamarind juice obtained from 1 tablespoon of tamarind pulp in 2 tablespoons of water.

Combine the Spice Paste, coconut cream, carambola, turmeric and "cup leaf" in a large bowl.

Spread the Spice Paste mixture over the fish before wrapping it with the banana leaf.

Glutinous Rice Flour Cakes (Lapek Bugis)

250 ml (1 cup) thick coconut milk
Pinch of salt
250 g (2 cups) white glutinous rice flour
125 g (1 cup) black glutinous rice flour (see note)
2 large banana leaves, softened (page 2) and cut into 18-cm (7-in) squares, for wrapping
300 ml (1$^1/_4$ cups) coconut cream
Toothpicks

Filling
200 g (2 cups) freshly grated coconut
150 g ($^3/_4$ cup) sugar
85 ml ($^1/_3$ cup) water
$^1/_2$ teaspoon vanilla essence

Makes 20 cakes
Preparation time: **40 mins**
Cooking time: **20 mins**

1 To make the Filling, stir-fry all the ingredients in a wok or skillet over medium heat until the mixture dries up, about 5 minutes. Remove and set aside.
2 Heat the coconut milk and salt in a saucepan over low heat, stirring continuously until the salt is dissolved, about 5 minutes. Remove and set aside to cool.
3 Combine both glutinous rice flour in a mixing bowl and mix well. Gradually stir in the salted coconut milk and mix into a smooth, non-sticky dough.
4 Flour your hands, pull out about 1 tablespoon of the dough and roll it into a small ball. Place the ball of dough on a piece of banana leaf and lightly press it with your hand to flatten, then roll it into a thin circle with a rolling pin. Place 1 tablespoon of the Filling onto the center of the circle and fold the edges up to neatly enclose the Filling, pressing at the seam to seal.
5 Spread 1 to 2 tablespoons of the coconut cream over the cake and fold the banana leaf in half to enclose the cake. Fold the corners inward at both ends, then fold both ends to the base and fasten the folded ends at the base with toothpicks, forming a package. Repeat until all the ingredients are used up.
6 Steam the cake packages in a steamer for 20 minutes.

If black glutinous rice flour is not available, soak 125 g ($^1/_2$ cup) black glutinous rice in water for 4 hours. Drain and grind with some coconut milk in a blender to a smooth paste. Combine with the white glutinous rice flour in step 3.

Roll the dough into a thin circle on a piece of banana leaf and top with 1 tablespoon of the Filling.

Fold the banana leaf in half to enclose the cake, then fold the corners inward at both ends.

Glutinous Rice with Fruit in Coconut Sauce (Nasi Tuai)

300 g (1$\frac{1}{2}$ cups) uncooked white glutinous rice,
  soaked in warm water for 2 hours and drained
2 pandanus leaves, raked with a fork
$\frac{1}{2}$ teaspoon salt
185 ml ($\frac{3}{4}$ cup) thick coconut milk

Coconut Sauce
750 ml (3 cups) thick coconut milk
185 g (1 cup) shaved palm sugar or dark brown sugar
1 to 2 tablespoons sugar
2 pandanus leaves, raked with a fork, tied into a knot
5 seeds ripe jackfruit or durian, seeds discarded, flesh sliced
2 eggs, lightly beaten (optional)

1 To make the Coconut Sauce, bring the coconut milk, sugar, pandanus leaves and fruit slices slowly to a boil over medium heat in a saucepan, stirring constantly. Simmer uncovered for 5 minutes and stir in the beaten eggs (if using). Remove from heat and discard the pandanus leaves. Set aside.
2 Line a steamer with a wet cloth and spread the glutinous rice evenly on top. Cover and steam for 20 minutes until cooked, then transfer to a large bowl.
3 Bring the pandanus leaves, salt and coconut milk to a boil over medium heat in a saucepan, stirring constantly. Simmer uncovered for 3 minutes and remove from heat. Discard the pandanus leaves, pour the fragrant coconut milk over the glutinous rice and mix thoroughly until the coconut milk is absorbed.
4 To serve, press some cooked glutinous rice firmly into a small bowl and invert it onto a serving plate, then spread the Coconut Sauce all around it.

If fresh jackfruit or durian are not available, you may use canned jackfruit or 2 fresh bananas.

Serves 4 to 6
Preparation time: **20 mins + 2 hours soaking**
Cooking time: **35 mins**

Pancakes with Coconut Sauce (Sarabi)

300 g (2¹/₂ cups) flour, sifted

2 eggs, lightly beaten

2 teaspoons instant yeast granules

300 ml (1¹/₄ cups) warm thick coconut milk

¹/₂ teaspoon vanilla essence

Pinch of salt

1 tablespoon oil or butter

Coconut Sauce

375 ml (1¹/₂ cups) thick coconut milk

185 g (1 cup) shaved palm sugar or dark brown sugar

1 to 2 tablespoons sugar

Pinch of salt

1 pandanus leaf, raked with a fork, tied into a knot

Serves 4 to 6
Preparation time: **20 mins** + **1 hour fermentation**
Cooking time: **30 mins**

1 To make the Coconut Sauce, combine all the ingredients in a saucepan and bring to a boil over medium heat, then reduce heat to low and simmer for 2 minutes, stirring constantly until all the sugar is dissolved. Remove and discard the pandanus leaf, and set aside.

2 Combine the flour, beaten eggs and yeast in a mixing bowl, and gradually stir in the warm coconut milk. Add the vanilla essence and salt, and mix into a thick smooth batter. Cover with a cloth and leave the batter to ferment in a warm place for 1 hour. The batter should turn fluffy when it is well fermented.

3 To make the pancakes, lightly grease a small wok or omelet pan with the oil or butter and heat over low heat. Once the wok or pan is hot, place a ladleful of the batter onto the wok or pan, turning to spread evenly. Cook for about 2 to 3 minutes until the pancake is set on top, then carefully turn it over with a spatula and cook the other side until golden brown. Remove and set aside. Repeat until all the batter is used up.

4 Pour some Coconut Sauce over each pancake and serve immediately.

These cakes are traditionally made using a small terracotta wok, but a metal wok is an adequate substitute.

Mix the mixture into a thick smooth batter and leave it in a warm place to ferment for 1 hour.

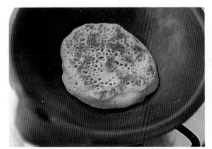

Once the pancake is set on top, turn it over and cook the other side until golden brown.

Steamed Rice Cake with Coconut Custard Topping (Sarimuko)

Rice Layer

300 g (1 1/2 cups) uncooked white glutinous rice, soaked in warm water for 2 hours and drained

125 ml (1/2 cup) coconut cream

1 pandanus leaf, raked with a fork, tied into a knot

Custard Topping

3 pandanus leaves, coarsely chopped

375 ml (1 1/2 cups) thick coconut milk

3 eggs

150 g (3/4 cup) sugar

5 tablespoons (50 g) rice flour

Pinch of salt

Makes 15 pieces
Preparation time: **20 mins + 2 hours soaking**
Cooking time: **1 hour**

1 To make the Rice Layer, place the glutinous rice in a cake pan. Add the coconut cream and pandanus leaf, and mix well, then steam in a steamer for 15 minutes. Remove and discard the pandanus leaf and continue to steam for another 10 minutes until cooked. Set aside to cool.

2 To make the Custard Topping, pulse the pandanus leaves with 1/2 of the coconut milk in a blender until finely chopped. Sieve the fragrant coconut milk into a bowl, pressing with a spoon to extract those trapped in the pandanus leaves. Set aside. Beat the eggs and sugar in a mixing bowl until the sugar is dissolved. Stir in the fragrant coconut milk and the remaining coconut milk and fold in the rice flour and salt until well blended.

3 Flake the Rice Layer with a fork and compress by pressing it with the back of a spoon. Pour the Custard Topping over the Rice Layer through a sieve. Return to the steamer, cover and steam for 30 minutes, until the topping is set. Remove and set aside to cool. Cut the rice cake into rectangular or diamond shapes to serve.

If the cake is steamed in a bamboo steamer basket, add boiling water to the wok every 10 minutes.

Sieve the fragrant coconut milk into a bowl, pressing with a spoon to extract.

Flake and compress the cooked glutinous rice, then pour the Custard Topping over it through a sieve.

Index